W9-AHP-849

We Work! Animals with Jobs

Homing Pigeons

by Jenny Fretland VanVoorst

Consultant:
Bonnie V. Beaver
College of Veterinary Medicine
Texas A&M University

BEARPORT
PUBLISHING

Credits

Cover and Title Page, © Michael Ninger/Shutterstock; 4–5, © guentermanaus/ Shutterstock; 6–7, © imago stock&people/Newscom; 8–9, © Jose Carlos Fajardo/MCT/ Newscom; 10, © Anita Huszti/Shutterstock; 10–11, © iStockphoto/Thinkstock; 12–13, © St Petersburg Times/ZUMA Press/Newscom; 14–15, © World History Archive/Newscom; 16, © Chandler NI Syndication/Newscom; 16–17, © Apic/Hulton Archive/Getty Images; 18–19, © Jim Damaske/ZUMA Press/Newscom; 20–21, © Richard Bedford/Alamy; 22T, © World History Archive/Newscom; 22B, © St Petersburg Times/ZUMA Press/Newscom; 23T, © Chandler NI Syndication/Newscom; 23B, © Dmitry Chernobrov/Shutterstock.

Publisher: Kenn Goin
Editor: Joyce Tavolacci
Creative Director: Spencer Brinker
Design: Craig Hinton
Photo Researcher: Arnold Ringstad

Library of Congress Cataloging-in-Publication Data

Fretland VanVoorst, Jenny, 1972–
  Homing pigeons / by Jenny Fretland VanVoorst.
      p. cm. — (We work!: Animals with jobs)
  Includes bibliographical references and index.
  ISBN-13: 978-1-61772-900-3 (library binding) — ISBN-10: 1-61772-900-0 (library binding)
  1. Homing pigeons—Juvenile literature. 2. Pigeons—Juvenile literature. 3. Working animals—Juvenile literature. I. Title.
  SF465.35.F74 2014
  636.5'96—dc23

                                        2013011059

For more information, write to Bearport Publishing Company, Inc., 45 West 21st Street, Suite 3B, New York, New York 10010. Printed in the United States of America.

10 9 8 7 6 5 4 3 2 1

Contents

Ace the Homing Pigeon

Meet Ace the **homing** pigeon.

He flies far to deliver messages for his owner.

Amazingly, this working bird never gets lost.

No matter where he is, Ace always knows how to get back home!

What Are Homers?

Homing pigeons are often called homers.

They look like common pigeons that live in the park.

Homers, however, have important jobs to do.

These special birds carry messages for people.

Message Received

Some people travel with their homing pigeons.

That way, they can send messages back home.

They attach a tiny note to the bird's leg.

Then the pigeon carries the message all the way home!

message

Far and Fast

Homers can travel far and fast.

They can fly more than 1,100 miles (1,770 km) in just two days.

They are also quick—as fast as a car on the highway!

On long trips, homers may stop and rest along the way.

Yet they always make it home.

Finding Their Way

How do homing pigeons find their way back home?

Scientists are not sure.

Some think the birds can smell their way home.

Others think that homers have a great sense of hearing.

This could help them pick up the familiar sounds of home.

pigeon
arriving home

A Long History

Homers have worked with people for thousands of years.

For most of that time, there were no phones or computers.

Instead, many people used pigeons to **communicate** with each other.

Using homers was often the fastest and easiest way to send messages.

15

Feathered Heroes

In the past, homers were used during war.

They carried messages between **soldiers**, such as "Help, we are under attack!"

Sometimes, the birds were shot at and **injured**.

soldier helping an injured pigeon

Some got awards for being brave.

soldier

Training

Homers are born with the skill to find their way home.

Yet they still need some training.

At first, owners take the pigeons a short distance from home and then release them.

Then, they take the birds farther and farther away.

With practice, the pigeons learn how to fly home—and get there fast!

owner training
a pigeon

Amazing Birds

Today, homing pigeons still help people communicate.

They sometimes carry notes between small villages in Asia.

Often, they are the fastest way to send messages.

Next time you see a pigeon in the sky, it might be a homer hard at work!

Glossary

communicate
(kuh-MYOO-nuh-kayt)
to pass on information

homing (HOH-ming)
able to find the way
home from a long
distance away

injured (IN-jurd)
hurt or damaged

soldiers
(SOUL-jurs)
people who
fight in wars

23

Index

Read More

Burleigh, Robert. *Fly, Cher Ami, Fly!: The Pigeon Who Saved the Lost Battalion.* New York: Abrams (2008).

Presnall, Judith Janda. *Carrier Pigeons (Animals with Jobs).* San Diego, CA: KidHaven (2004).

Learn More Online

To learn more about homing pigeons, visit **www.bearportpublishing.com/WeWork**

About the Author

Jenny Fretland VanVoorst is a writer and editor of books for young people. She enjoys learning about all kinds of topics. When she is not reading and writing, Jenny enjoys kayaking, playing the piano, and watching wildlife. She lives in Minneapolis, Minnesota, with her husband, Brian, and their two pets.